"This kind can onl

Mark 9:29

Only by Prayer

When God Breaks Through

Study Guide

David Gudgel, Steve Durand, Dan Stockum

Co-authors

ONLY BY PRAYER
Copyright © 2019 David Gudgel, Steve Durand, and Dan Stockum
Printed by Kindle Direct Publishing
https://kdp.amazon.com

Library of Congress Cataloging-in-Publication Data
Gudgel, David, Steve Durand, and Dan Stockum
Only by Prayer / David Gudgel, Steve Durand, and Dan Stockum
Includes bibliographical .

ISBN: 9781795009379

Contents

Introduction

If there is an area in your life where you are longing for a breakthrough but it's just not happening, it could be that there is a barrier of some kind between you and God that is preventing Him from doing what you can't do on your own.

It could be that you just need to *ask* Him. That's what James said. "You have not, because you ask not" (James 4:2b). Our all-knowing, all-powerful, all-loving heavenly Father may simply be waiting for you to come before His throne of grace, in your time of need, and ask for His help with something that you can't do in your own strength.

That's part of the problem, isn't it? *Our* strength. *Our* ingenuity. *Our* independence. That's what we've chased our whole life. It's what our parents wanted for us – that we would grow up to be responsible, independent, hardworking, successful adults. And all of that is obviously a good thing in this world. But...

God wants us, as we grow to be *independent* of our parents, to also grow more and more *dependent* on Him. He wants us to understand that we can't do this on our own. He wants His children to come to Him in prayer, again and again, and seek His help, wisdom, peace, provision, plans, power, and more.

This lesson isn't easily learned, especially in our self-sufficient "we can do this" world. Even Jesus' disciples learned this lesson the hard way. After failure. They were trying to do miracles – which they had done before – but now it wasn't working. They were confused. And when they asked Jesus about it, He replied,

This kind can only come out by prayer.
Mark 9:29

Introduction

The disciples had started out depending on God's power to work through them, and they saw amazing things happen. But they had become confident in themselves as time went on, and forgot that it was God alone who could do the impossible.

God wants us to come to Him in prayer and ask for His help.

But simply asking is not enough. Simply coming to God and saying, "I need you to fix this" is not enough. *How* we ask is important too. What's going on in our hearts and minds and lives matters.

That's what we will be looking at in this *Only by Prayer* study over the course of the next forty days. We will look at some of the barriers that could be keeping you from seeing God work mightily in your life. We will think about how God wants you to pray to ask for His help, so that He will intervene and help you break through those areas of need that you are struggling with in your life.

It is our hope that God will use this study over the next forty days to infuse your prayer life with new power and passion, and as a result, that you will see God's hand working mightily in and through your life.

How to Use this Study Guide

Only by Prayer is a six-week study. To compliment the messages that will be taught in our worship services, this study guide will help you dig deeper into each week's topic as you (1) attend a weekly small group and then (2) follow along with your own personal devotions each day. Though we would encourage you to join a small group, if that isn't possible, the Introduction to each week and the Personal Daily Devotions can also be used on their own.

This study guide contains the following for each of the six weeks:

- **Introduction** – This information will help you focus on the topic for the week.

- **Video notes** – Each session includes a video for your small group to watch together. Pages are provided in this study guide that you can use to take notes during the videos.

- **Questions for Group Discussion** – After watching the video, questions are provided for you to discuss with your small group, that will take you deeper into the topic. Don't feel like you have to answer all the questions. Let the video notes and the questions lead you into a time of learning and exhortation and encouragement together.

- **Personal Daily Devotions** – There are Personal Daily Devotions at the end of each session in this study guide. Whether you are in a small group or not, these daily devotions will help you think deeper about your own prayer life and the things that might be standing in the way of personal breakthroughs.

Also included in this study guide:

- **Resources for Group Leaders** – Information that will help those who are leading small groups through this study.

- **Answers** for video notes

- **Weekly Family Devotions** – Six lessons with ideas you can use each week to study *Only by Prayer* with your family.

Week 1

Reliant

"Teacher, I brought you my son, who is possessed by a spirit that has robbed him of speech. Whenever it seizes him, it throws him to the ground. He foams at the mouth, gnashes his teeth and becomes rigid. I asked your disciples to drive out the spirit, but they could not." ... But Jesus took him by the hand and lifted him to his feet, and he stood up. After Jesus had gone indoors, his disciples asked him privately, "Why couldn't we drive it out?" He replied, "This kind can come out only by prayer." – Mark 9:17b,18,27-29

Day 1: Introduction to Week 1

Reliant: adjective
Dependent on someone or something

The early church was BIG on prayer. It wasn't just a second thought or a nice thing to do every now and then. It was an essential, because they knew they were totally dependent on God's leading and His power. For the early church, prayer was a vital part of the life-changing work that God did in and through His followers from Jerusalem to the uttermost parts of the world.

Before the 1st church became a church, they prayed. Constantly!

> *Acts 1:13-14 – When they arrived, they went upstairs to the room where they were staying. Those present were Peter, John, James and Andrew; Philip and Thomas, Bartholomew and Matthew; James son of Alphaeus and Simon the Zealot, and Judas son of James. They all joined together **constantly in prayer,** along with the women and Mary the mother of Jesus, and with his brothers.*

After the early church began, they prayed. Constantly!

> *Acts 2:42 – And they were **continually devoting** them-selves to the apostles' teaching and to fellowship, to the breaking of bread and **to prayer.***

As the church grew, their leaders prayed. Constantly!

> *Acts 6:4 – We will **continue steadfastly in prayer,** and in the ministry of the word. (ASV)*

When the church faced persecution, they prayed. Constantly!

> *Acts 12:5 – While Peter was being kept in jail, the church **never stopped praying** to God for him.*

Do you see a pattern? The early church prayed about everything. Prayer was their lifeblood. Prayer was foremost in their minds. They knew they could not be the church the Lord intended for them to be without prayer. They not only believed that, they constantly practiced that. They relied on the One who could do what they could not do, through prayer.

For the early church, prayer was more than just something they should do. It was something they did. Constantly!

God can do what you and I can't. And the key that unlocks God doing what only God can do, is prayer.

That belief profoundly influenced A.C. Dixon, popular 19th century Pastor and Evangelist, who said...

"When we rely on organization, we get what organization can do; when we rely on education, we get what education can do; when we rely on eloquence, we get what eloquence can do; and so on. I am not disposed to undervalue any of these things in their proper place—But when we rely on prayer, we get what God can do."

That's what we want, isn't it? God doing what we can't. Beyond what we could ask or think. That's possible because nothing is impossible with God.

That breakthrough you need – God can bring it. The closed door you can't open – God can make a way. That relationship that's broken – God can mend it. That disaster that undid years of building and sacrifice – God can restore what has been lost.

How? Reliant prayer.

That breakthrough you need could be just a prayer away.

Watch Video 1   **Reliant**

Your notes:

_____

_____

_____

_____

Nehemiah relied on prayer:

1. _____ the wall was rebuilt

   Nehemiah 1:4 – When I heard these things, I sat down and wept. For some days I mourned and fasted and prayed before the God of heaven.

2. _____ the wall was rebuilt

   Nehemiah 4:4a – Hear us, O our God, for we are despised. Turn their insults back on their own heads...

3. _____ the wall was rebuilt

   Nehemiah 9:5b-6a – Blessed be your glorious name, and may it be exalted above all blessing and praise. You alone are the LORD.

Questions for Group Discussion

1. In what ways do you identify with Nehemiah's prayer life?

2. Life is a series of before, during, and after circumstances. In which seasons are you most and least likely to turn to prayer? What does that tell you about your viewpoint on prayer?

3. Prayer for Nehemiah was a non-negotiable. Especially when things were tough (as you can see in Nehemiah 2:4; 4:4-5,9; 5:19; 6:9,14). How did Nehemiah's prayer in the middle of hardship impact his and the wall-builders' attitudes?

4. As was said on page 9, the early church constantly prayed. They relied on prayer, like Nehemiah did, for whatever they faced, whenever they faced it. What can be done to keep this timeless practice central in our lives in the 21st century?

5. How do you hope to be impacted by this 40-day *Only by Prayer* series? What breakthroughs would you like to see happen in your life because of what you learn and practice during this time?

Week 1

Personal Daily Devotions

Reliant

O my God, I trust, lean on, rely on,
and am confident in You.

Psalm 25:2

Day 2

Even Jesus relied on frequent times of prayer

But Jesus often withdrew to lonely places and prayed.
Luke 5:16

Think about the things you rely on: coffee, sleep, food, payday, a car, parents, your toothbrush. All too important to do without. That's what prayer was to Jesus. From the start to the finish of His earthly ministry, Jesus relied on prayer. Every word of Luke 5:16 tells us that.

But Jesus, in spite of His growing popularity and the increasing demands being placed on Him, made time for prayer. It remained central in His life and His ministry. Jesus constantly prayed.

Often. Frequently. Intentionally. Like we regularly eat, Jesus regularly prayed. Like any strong relationship, the Father and Son talked a lot. Jesus' day-to-day life was filled with frequent, intentional times when He prayed.

Withdrew to lonely places. Even Jesus needed times of solitude with His Heavenly Father. He intentionally set aside time to step away from everything else to talk to God. No phones, no television, no needy people, no chores. Just Jesus and God the Father. Sometimes He went alone out into the beauty of God's creation. At other times He simply took advantage of the quiet hours of the night or early morning. Simply to be alone with God.

And prayed. Jesus talked to God and listened to God. He held nothing back. He aligned His will to His Father's will. He gave thanks. He prayed for others. He prayed for help. He asked for guidance. He prayed like we need to pray, about everything.

We need to rely on prayer like Jesus did.

Your Personal Reflection and Application

If Jesus relied on prayer, we should too. Think about your attitude toward prayer. In your normal, day-to-day life is it something you literally depend on, or just something you do occasionally?

_____

_____

Jesus took time to pray. Do you have specific time in your days set aside for prayer? If not, when are some times that you could set aside for prayer? What do you need to do to make that happen?

_____

_____

Jesus went to places where He could be alone with God. What lonely places do you have in your life where you can go for times of solitude and prayer? How does thinking about these times make you feel?

_____

_____

When you pray, what do you usually focus on? Are there certain things you always pray about? What more would you pray about if you actually took the time?

_____

_____

Day 3

Abraham was at his best when he relied on God

There Abram called on the name of the Lord.
Genesis 13:4

Many of us rely on our smartphones for pretty much everything! It's our phone, camera, calendar, clock, maps and directions, games, shopping, texts and video chats, rides to the airport... The thought of going without our phone, even for an hour or two, doesn't even cross our minds. We need it every hour!

We need to rely on prayer even more.

Abraham built a lot of altars during his lifetime, where he called on the name of the Lord. He usually built these altars each time God led him to a new place. Like when God relocated him from Haran to Canaan, and *"he built an altar to the Lord, who had appeared to him"* (Genesis 12:7). He built another altar after he moved to Bethel and *"there Abram called on the name of the Lord"* (Genesis 12:8). Later, he came back to the altar that was still standing at Bethel and again *"called on the name of the Lord"* (Genesis 13:4). After a move to Hebron, *"he built an altar to the Lord there"* (Genesis 13:18). It's likely Abraham also built an altar at Beersheba where he *"called upon the name of the Lord, the Eternal God"* (Genesis 21:33).

It's interesting to note two times when he *didn't* build an altar. In Egypt (Genesis 12) and in Gerar (Genesis 20). Both of those times he ended up relying on deception instead of on God, when he told Sarah to lie for their protection. He relied on his own schemes instead of on God.

Like Abraham, we need to remind ourselves through times of prayer that we can and should rely on God for everything.

Your Personal Reflection and Application

Who do you most often rely on for help? How do you usually contact them and how often?

_____

_____

_____

When you look at the current state of your life and your prayers, would you say it reflects a person that is more dependent on God or on yourself? How so?

_____

_____

_____

Why does sin often follow a lack of reliance upon God? How can prayer keep us from falling into sin?

_____

_____

_____

Abraham built altars as a way to demonstrate his reliance on God. What type of "altars" do you, or could you, build in your life for the same purpose?

_____

_____

_____

Day 4

Victory came when King Asa relied on the Lord

Then Asa called to the LORD his God and said, "LORD, there is no one besides You to help in the battle between the powerful and those who have no strength; so help us, O LORD our God, for we trust in You..." So the LORD routed the Ethiopians before Asa and before Judah, and the Ethiopians fled. – 2 Chronicles 14:11-12

Life has a way of bringing us to our knees, and when it does the best thing we can do is what King Asa did when he faced insurmountable odds. He turned to the Lord for help.

Asa enjoyed ten years of peace at the beginning of his 41-year reign as King over Judah. But peace disappeared when General Zerah attacked Asa's half-million-man army with his million-man army. Humanly speaking, the odds of victory weren't on Asa's side. But the Lord supernaturally intervened and gave Asa a never-to-be forgotten victory and lesson – the Lord is capable of doing what you can't. Always seek the Lord's help. Always!

Unfortunately, a quarter of a century later, when Asa was faced with a new military threat and a deadly disease, he forgot that lesson and did not seek help from the Lord (2 Chronicles 16:7,12). Instead, he relied on human ingenuity (a bribe and treaty) and human intervention (physicians). Both were to Asa's undoing in the final five years of his life.

Though we can find help of a kind from man, the blight against Asa was that *"he **did not** seek help from the Lord, but **only** from the physicians"* (2 Chronicles 16:12). And just like Asa, we can all make the mistake of relying on man and his wisdom instead of on God.

We need to remember that above all else, our help is from the Lord. We should call out to Him and rely on Him.

Your Personal Reflection and Application

What circumstances have come into your life that would have been to your undoing had you not relied on the Lord?

_____

_____

_____

How have you seen the Lord almighty intervene in your life in ways that showed His greatness?

_____

_____

_____

Have you in the past or present fallen into the "I can take care of this myself" trap before turning to God for help? Why do we often wait and only turn to God as a last resort?

_____

_____

_____

What do you need to remember, or do, to make turning to God for help your first response instead of trying to figure it out for yourself first?

_____

_____

_____

Day 5

Daniel, in the face of death, kept on praying

"Anyone who makes a petition to any god or man besides you, O king, for thirty days, shall be cast into the lions' den"... Now when Daniel learned that the decree had been published, he went home to his upstairs room where the windows opened toward Jerusalem. Three times a day he got down on his knees and prayed, giving thanks to his God, just as he had done before. – Daniel 6:7,10

Daniel could have put his prayer life on pause for 30-days, like we might take a break from a diet during the holidays. "Eating healthy is important," we say, "but not during the holidays." We know we can enjoy all the special treats and then jump back into the diet after the holidays are over.

If ever there was what seemed like a good reason to take a vacation from prayer – at least from outward postures of prayer that others could see – you'd think the threat of death by lions would be the one. After all, Daniel could still be praying on the inside even though it didn't look like it on the outside, or he could find a secret place where no one could see him praying.

So, what did Daniel do? Pray one more time that God would understand why he needed to take a 30-day break from his normal routine of prayer? No.

Even in the face of death, Daniel continued praying *"as he had done before"* with windows wide open, down on his knees, praising God and asking for His help (Daniel 6:10-11).

Daniel knew that he needed God's help, every day. And he wanted everyone to know that his relationship with God was more important than any decree from any earthly king. He knew his very life was in God's hands alone.

Your Personal Reflection and Application

Put yourself in Daniel's shoes. Based on your present commitment to prayer, would you have continued praying in the face of the death threat Daniel faced?

_____

_____

_____

What does the frequency of your prayer life tell you about the depth of your reliance on God?

_____

_____

_____

When it comes to praying in public, do you? What often stands in the way of God's children praying in bold ways?

_____

_____

_____

Some things in life are too important to neglect even for a day or two. What things in your life would be on that list? How can you make sure prayer is one of those things?

_____

_____

_____

Day 6

Paul relied on prayer when he couldn't be there

Night and day we pray most earnestly that we may see you again and supply what is lacking in your faith.
1 Thessalonians 3:10

One of the best ways to show your love and concern for someone, especially when you're separated by distance, is to pray for them. You can always rely on prayer when you can't be there. Paul did.

From what we know, Paul didn't spend much time in the thriving city of Thessalonica. Probably less than a month. But during his brief time there he developed a deep love for the believers he met there. So much so that he longed to be with them again. But in spite of his repeated efforts to return and care for these new babes in Christ, he was prevented from making the 150-mile trip.

So Paul did what we can do when we're apart from those we love dearly. He relied on prayer. He prayed night and day for them. Earnestly. He put his heart into frequent, fervent, faithful prayers. Paul's prayer life was the real thing. He prayed for Timothy night and day (2 Timothy 1:3). He constantly prayed for the church at Rome (Romans 1:9). He did what he told others to do: pray at all times (Ephesians 6:18); pray without ceasing (1 Thessalonians 5:17); be devoted to prayer (Romans 12:12).

Paul relied on prayer when he could not be there. He turned to the One who could do more than he could do even if he was there. In the same way, when we rely on prayer, we rely on the One who can do what we can't, and more.

As we are apart from those that we love, let's lift them up to God regularly and passionately in times of prayer. Let's entrust them to the One who is with them, even when we're not.

Your Personal Reflection and Application

Who would you like to be with right now, but you can't?

_____

_____

_____

In what ways have you benefited by the prayers of others who were unable to be personally with you? How did knowing that others were praying impact you?

_____

_____

_____

When someone fervently prays about someone or something – night and day, constantly – what does that tell you about their beliefs about prayer?

_____

_____

_____

In what ways do you rely on prayer? In what ways is your prayer life like, or unlike, the Apostle Paul?

_____

_____

_____

Day 7

Application Day: Your reliant prayer plan

As we saw this week on Day 5, even in the face of death Daniel did not put his prayer life on hold for 30-days. But instead he continued to pray "...*just as he had done before*" (Daniel 6:10).

If you were to continue to pray "just as you have done before" over the remaining 33 days of our *Only by Prayer* focus, what would your prayer life look like? (Be specific...)

_____

_____

_____

_____

This would be a good time to stop and ask God what He would have you do that would increase your reliance on Him through prayer. As far as your personal prayers go, what are you currently doing that you'd like to keep doing, and what would you like to add during the remaining 33 days that you are not yet doing?

_____

_____

_____

_____

Think about the people and circumstances in your life right now that you want to bring before God for His help. Write them on the following chart and then use it as a reminder to pray, relying on God to answer.

Record your 33-day prayer plan below

Sun	Mon	Tue	Wed	Thu	Fri	Sat

Week 2

Repentant

He who conceals his sins does not prosper,
but whoever confesses and renounces them finds mercy.

Proverbs 28:13

Day 8: Introduction to Week 2

I was wrong. I have sinned. I am sorry. Please forgive me.

Those might be some of the most difficult sentences for us to say, but as we will see this week, they can be some of the most needed for breakthroughs.

Repentant prayer is, at a minimum, what is classically called "the sinner's prayer." We acknowledge before God that we have sinned against Him and ask for forgiveness.

Contrary to what some people may believe, this is not simply a one-time confession when we initially ask Christ for forgiveness and become a Christian. Instead, this is an ongoing, necessary practice in the life of every faithful Christian.

Because God loves us, repentant prayer is necessary to move forward with Him whether we have been a Christian for five minutes or fifty-five years. He cares too much for us to lead us into deeper spiritual depths when we continue to ignore glaring sin in our lives.

Once we can admit our problem and ask for forgiveness, the sin no longer stands in the way between us and where God wants to lead us. Of course, even with repentant prayer, breakthrough may not immediately arrive. But we know for sure that without repentant prayer, breakthrough will certainly never arrive.

This week, prepare to face and own up to your shortcomings. Allow God to probe deep into your heart to uncover both your obvious and your not so obvious sin. Don't fear this. It is the loving work of a God who wants you to move forward. With repentant prayer, you'll find that you have nothing to lose and everything to gain.

Watch Video 2   Repentant

Your notes:

_____

_____

_____

_____

1. **Before** praying repentantly...

   If we avoid confession, it leads to _____

2. **After** praying repentantly...

   We experience _____ and _____

3. God will _____, _____, and
   _____ us in the way we should go

Questions for Group Discussion

1. What is your experience with repenting? Is it difficult for you? How often do you find yourself repenting?

2. Do you tend to put any qualifiers on your repentance such as, "Yes, I was wrong, but only because," or, "I wouldn't have if he hadn't…"

3. During the seasons of your life when you were avoiding repentance, how did it feel to have something covered up?

4. What are the typical ways in which you try to "hide" when you have shame?

5. How has it felt to confess in the past?

6. What makes repentance easier?

7. What are the benefits of repenting that you have experienced? What are the costs that you have found if you don't repent?

Week 2

Personal Daily Devotions

Repentant

He who conceals his sins does not prosper,
but whoever confesses and renounces them finds mercy.

Proverbs 28:13

Day 9

Repentant Prayer is a Gift, Granted by God

"God exalted Him (Christ) to His own right hand as Prince and Savior that He might give repentance and forgiveness of sins to Israel." —Acts 5:31

"So then, God has granted even the Gentiles repentance onto life." —Acts 11:17-18

"Opponents must be gently instructed, in the hope that God will grant them repentance leading them to a knowledge of the truth, and that they will come to their senses and escape from the trap of the devil, who has taken them captive to do his will." —2 Timothy 2:23-26

In yesterday's introduction, we said that without repentant prayer, breakthrough will be impossible. Today, we ask the question, "What if you are in a season when you know you are pursuing sin, but you are not convicted enough to genuinely ask for forgiveness and turn from that sin?"

In other words, what can you do when you have no desire to stop sinning in a particular area?

You can ask God to grant you repentance.

If you want a relationship with God, but you want a relationship with a particular sin even more, you can ask God to grant you repentance. If you know in your head what you are doing is wrong, but you don't know it in your heart and have no motivation to turn from it, you can ask God to grant you repentance.

Even if you aren't currently consciously running from God, there are always some areas of our hearts, perhaps unknown to us, that desire something more than God. Ask God to reveal these areas to you and grant you repentance.

Where would you place yourself right now? Is your heart broken in all of the same ways that God's is? Are there aspects of your life that you know are out of line with God's commands yet you aren't bothered enough to stop sinning?

If so, pray "Lord bring me to repentance. Show me the depth of my errors. Help me to grieve as You do when I reject You or Your ways, and then help me turn from them."

Your Personal Reflection and Application

When have you typically felt remorse for your sinful actions? When have you known that you were behaving sinfully yet felt no remorse?

_____

_____

_____

What has helped move you toward remorse for your sinful actions in the past? Have you ever asked God to grant you repentance?

_____

_____

_____

_____

Day 10

Repentant Prayer is Humble

"If My people, who are called by My name, will humble themselves and pray and seek My face and turn from their wicked ways, then will I hear from heaven and will forgive their sin and will heal their land."
2 Chronicles 7:14

"God opposes the proud but gives grace to the humble."
1 Peter 5:5

Though we may try, with God we can never barter. With God, we can never demand. With God, we never have the upper hand. With God, we come as undeserving beggars, or we do not come at all. There is no other choice.

Our ways have been wicked, and even our righteousness is tainted with sin (Isaiah 64:6) so that we cannot stand before God on our own merits. We stand before Him only by depending on His mercy and the status He has given us through Christ.

In other words, we approach Him in prayer with a humble attitude. We approach Him repentantly. We know the only reason He will listen to us is because of His grace toward us -- not because we have earned a right to ask anything of Him.

Is this how you begin your prayers? Are you typically in line with the Lord's Prayer which reads, *"Forgive us our sins as we forgive those who sin against us"*? Do you take time to repent by kneeling in wonder that God will hear your prayers?

Or do you perhaps believe that God owes you because of what you have done for Him? Or can you sometimes feel as though

God has given you a raw deal? That He has given others more than He has given you, and it's not fair?

If so, pride has clouded you from seeing your true position before God, and you need repentant prayer. God does not take orders. He only takes requests. There is no other way.

Your Personal Reflection and Application

When was the last time you prayed with an awareness that God was listening purely as an act of His grace?

_____

_____

_____

_____

_____

_____

What demands do you find yourself making of God?

_____

_____

_____

_____

_____

_____

Day 11

Repentant Prayer is Corporate

*"I am too ashamed and disgraced, my God, to lift up
my face to You, because our sins are higher than our
heads and our guilt has reached to the heavens."*
Ezra 9:6 (read 9:6-15)

*"Now, Lord our God, Who brought Your people out of Egypt
with a mighty hand and Who made for Yourself a name that
endures to this day, we have sinned, we have done wrong."*
Daniel 9:15 (read 9:4-19)

Ezra and Daniel were not only grieved over their own
wrongdoing, they were grieved that the corporate body, of
which they were a part, had disobeyed God. There is no evidence
to suggest that either Ezra or Daniel were directly involved in the
sins which the body at large had committed, and yet they
included themselves in the guilt of the group and asked for
forgiveness. *"We have sinned"* and *"our sins are higher than our
heads."*

Have you prayed like this? When you see wrongdoing in our
country, our state, or our church, do you pray "God forgive us
because we have sinned," or do you excuse yourself of guilt
because you believe only the "others" who were directly
involved are responsible?

Notice that neither Ezra nor Daniel pray "Lord, please forgive
them for not being as wise and holy as me." Instead, they take
the full measure of guilt incurred and declare themselves equally
liable.

Ezra and Daniel show us that since we are all part of the same
body, we cannot as a hand (for example) claim that the foot was

at fault while exempting ourselves. If one part of the body is sinful, all parts of the body are sinful.

Your Personal Reflection and Application

What are the glaringly obvious sins you see in the church? Do you tend to think "I wish they wouldn't do that?" Or do you think "I wish we wouldn't do that?"

_____

_____

_____

_____

_____

_____

How would taking responsibility for the sinful actions of the group influence how you pray for the church and how you work toward change in the group?

_____

_____

_____

_____

_____

_____

Day 12

Repentant Prayer is Sorrowful & Leads to Salvation

"Godly sorrow brings repentance that leads to salvation and leaves no regret, but worldly sorrow brings death. See what this godly sorrow has produced in you: what earnestness, what eagerness to clear yourselves, what indignation, what alarm, what longing, what concern, what readiness to see justice done."
2 Corinthians 7:10-11

If our prayers are repentant, our emotions will be involved and can be a helpful self-check as we evaluate if we are praying repentantly or not. If we offer up a simple "Sorry, God," without much contrition in our souls, we haven't really prayed repentantly. At the same time, if our prayers sound something like "If only I hadn't done that, everything would still be okay. But now, it's all ruined," we might be praying with worldly sorrow instead of repentance.

In a truly repentant prayer, we will feel indignation and alarm over our sin, which leads to both thanking God for the gift of salvation and a longing to set right what we have wounded.

In the old prayer books, confession of sin was always followed by praises for forgiveness, meaning that if we look at our sin and don't feel grateful for salvation, we've probably missed something.

At the same time, if looking at our sin doesn't provoke us to seek ways to restore what we have broken, we will also know that we missed repentant prayer.

As you pray over your sin, what emotions do you typically feel? Only regret or shame? If so, pray today that God would grant you eyes to see the depth of your salvation that you may praise Him for the forgiveness He has given you. Also pray that God would give you concern and longing to mend what your sin has torn apart.

It is entirely possible two of the breakthroughs God wants for you are (1) freeing you from the weight of worldly sorrow and regret and (2) moving you to action to repair the damage your sin has caused in your life and the lives of others.

Your Personal Reflection and Application

Do you typically pray with worldly sorrow that leads to regret, or with godly sorrow that leads to repentance and salvation?

_____

_____

_____

_____

_____

What are the influences that make you experience one versus the other?

_____

_____

_____

_____

_____

Day 13

Repentant Prayer Requires Others

"Therefore, confess your sins to one another and pray for one another, that you may be healed."
James 5:16

James shows us that repentant prayer cannot be completed alone. We will actually need another person to help us, and that person must know the sin that is truly happening in our lives.

For most of us, confessing our sins to another person and having that person pray for us will be the most difficult step in repentant prayer. Commonly, it seems easier to talk about our sin to God that it does to confess it to other people.

But confess it to others we must if we want to follow God's design for repentant prayer.

We might wonder, why would God want us to go through this excruciating step? Why isn't He satisfied with our private repentant prayer?

Because He wants us to be healed, James tells us. Healing comes through sharing our struggle with others and having them pray for us. While forgiveness comes through confessing to God and faith in Christ, healing seems to require other people and their prayers. Breakthrough may not come another way.

Is there a current or past sin you haven't confessed to anyone else? Can you see ways in which you have been or are still wounded by that sin? Do you perhaps carry around guilt for it? Did that sin begin a series of other bad decisions whose consequences are still felt in your life today?

We don't know what breakthrough God could bring in our lives through repentant prayer, and we won't know unless we confess to others and ask them to pray over us.

Your Personal Reflection and Application

Is confessing your sin to other people and having them pray over you a regular part of your life? If not, list the names of some people to whom you would be willing to confess. Pray over this list and seek God's leading to help you identify who might become that person for you.

_____

_____

_____

_____

_____

_____

What healing have you experienced from confessing your sin to another person and having that person pray for you?

_____

_____

_____

_____

_____

Days 14

Application Day: Next steps in Repentance

We have talked extensively about the importance of repentant prayer. Hopefully, after five days of devotions and prayer around the topic, God has moved in your heart. Now it is time to act.

Has God brought any personal, ongoing sin to your attention this week?

_____

What pride have you discovered in your prayers? In what ways do you presume God owes you something?

_____

What are the sins of your family, small group, church, city, and nation? Are you ready to stand before God and share the guilt of your community?

_____

What previously concealed sin is God showing you to confess to someone else in order for that person to pray for you?

_____

Have you identified a person to whom you can transparently confess your sin and ask for prayer?

_____

The next step is to confess to that person your previously unrevealed sin. This could mean confessing a sin for which you only recently felt conviction. Or confessing inappropriate attitudes when you pray. Or confessing a past or present sin you have never shared with anyone.

After meeting with that person, record some of your thoughts below:

How did you feel about contacting the person? Scared? Excited? Nervous?

_____

_____

As you confessed to the person, what were some of your thoughts and feelings? When you admitted that you needed prayer, were you filled with humility? When the person saw you for who you really are, were you filled with godly sorrow that led you to gratefulness for salvation or were you filled with worldly sorrow that led to shame and regret?

_____

_____

After you confessed and the person prayed for you, how did you feel? What are some of your new thoughts on the practice of confession, repentance, and prayer for one another?

_____

_____

If the person you chose did not clearly state the Gospel in their prayer as a response to your confession, hear it now and make this your prayer:

> God accepts me. I might sometimes feel like no one
> can accept me because of what I've done, but that's
> not true. Jesus paid the price for my sin. I am clean.
> I am loved. I am welcomed into His heavenly arms,
> and He will never let me go. I am free.

Week 3

Desperate

As the deer pants for streams of water,
so my soul pants for you, O God.

Psalm 42:1

Day 15: Introduction to Week 3

Committed. Generous. Gifted. Loving. Selfless. Encouraging.
A student of God's Word. Full of faith.

Most followers of Christ would love to be described by others in
any of these ways. But what if someone were to describe you as
desperate?

Desperation typically has a negative connotation in our world.
When we think about someone who is desperate, we likely think
about someone who is needy. Incapable. Weak. Helpless.
Hopeless.

Who wants to be thought of like that?

What we often fail to grasp, however, is that we *are* desperate.
Apart from God, we *are* needy. We *are* incapable. We *are* weak
and helpless and, yes, even hopeless.

We forget that, prior to coming to faith in Jesus, we were
completely without hope, dead in our transgressions and sins, far
away from God, and deserving of His wrath. We forget that we
can only come to God through His great mercy and grace, rather
than through any goodness or virtue of our own (Ephesians 2:1-
13).

Here's the point. Even though all of us *are* desperately needy and
hopeless apart from God, we all too frequently live or pretend as
if we're not. We want people to see us as self-sufficient and
capable, not desperate.

Is it possible, though, that God is simply waiting for you to fully
accept and embrace your desperate condition and to stop
leaning on your own understanding and resources, so that He
can finally bring about the breakthrough in your life and in the
church for which you've been waiting and hoping?

Watch Video 3   Desperate

Your notes:

_____

_____

_____

_____

What keeps us from being more desperate for God?

1. _____

2. _____

3. _____

Personal Response:

1. What did you hear?

_____

_____

2. How do you hope to respond?

_____

_____

Questions for Group Discussion

1. Talk about a season of life when you were desperate for help. Did you feel like you grew closer to God through that experience? Why or why not?

2. Do you feel the concept of being desperate for God is biblical? Why or why not?

3. In your own words, what does it mean to be desperate for God?

4. How might desperate prayer lead to spiritual breakthroughs?

5. Which of the three reasons for why we may not be more desperate for God (as discussed in the video) can you identify with the most?

6. Are there any additional reasons (not mentioned in the video) that you can think of as to why we're often not more desperate for God?

7. In what ways might prayer in desperate times help to ignite your faith?

8. After watching the video, what has God brought to your mind in terms of a next-step of application that you can take this week?

Week 3

Personal Daily Devotions

Desperate

As the deer pants for streams of water,
so my soul pants for you, O God.

Psalm 42:1

Day 16

Spiritually Poor

*"Blessed are the poor in spirit,
for theirs is the kingdom of heaven."*
Matthew 5:3

It's hard to admit that we don't have it all together. It's hard to ask for help. It's hard to admit that there are things we don't know, don't understand, or can't do.

Nevertheless, today's verse is a good reminder that God looks with favor upon those who recognize their utter need for Him. The question is whether or not you're willing to admit it and to live accordingly. If so, that's what it means to be *poor in spirit.* It's another way of saying that you're *desperate.* It's to recognize that, because of your sin, you are spiritually and hopelessly bankrupt before God. It's to humbly confess, "God, without You, I can do nothing and I am nothing. All of my hope is in you." And this verse teaches that it's only when you come to this realization and to this place of surrender that you are able to receive salvation (the kingdom of heaven) and to experience the spiritual riches that God offers to His children (Ephesians 1:3).

The reason why this matter is so important – particularly within the context of this study – is because there is a fundamental connection between desperation and prayer. Simply put, the more desperate (or poor in spirit) we realize we are, the more we will pray. And the more we pray and turn to God in desperation, the more we will come to know Him, to feel His presence, and possibly even begin to see Him bring about a breakthrough in our circumstances.

Your Personal Reflection and Application

Are you ever reluctant to ask for help or to reveal weakness to others? Why is that?

_____

_____

_____

_____

How does recognition and acceptance of our desperate condition drive us to prayer?

_____

_____

_____

_____

_____

How can you remind yourself this week of your desperate need for God?

_____

_____

_____

_____

_____

Day 17

A Desperate Prayer

"The Pharisee stood by himself and prayed, 'God I thank you that I am not like other people – robbers, evildoers, adulterers – or even like this tax collector. I fast twice a week and give a tenth of all I get.' But the tax collector stood at a distance. He would not even look up to heaven, but beat his breast and said, 'God, have mercy on me, a sinner.'"

Luke 18:11-13

It's easy to fall into the trap of just going through the motions of prayer. We get distracted, letting our minds wander, perhaps as we think about all of the things we need to do that day. And before we know it, prayer becomes just another routine. We forget what a privilege it is to pray. We forget that we're talking to the sovereign God of the universe, and that He is more interested in our hearts as we pray than He is in our words. We forget just how desperate and helpless we are before Him.

The tax collector to whom Jesus referred in today's theme verse, however, seemed to be keenly aware of his desperate condition. He didn't appear to be going through the motions with God. He made no excuses and didn't try to rationalize his sin. He didn't try to justify himself by talking about how much more righteous he was compared to others. In his eyes he was deserving of judgment, so he threw himself on the mercy of God.

When was the last time you prayed with that type of desperation? When was the last time you pinned all of your hopes on God, humbly acknowledging that there's no one and nowhere else to turn but to Him? Why not start today?

Your Personal Reflection and Application

How can you tell when you're just going through the motions of prayer?

_____

_____

_____

_____

Where do you see the separate attitudes and approaches of the Pharisee and the tax collector in today's Bible passage operating in your own life?

_____

_____

_____

_____

How does this story illustrate that spiritual desperation is not so much a conscious choice as it is an attitude that organically arises when we come to grips with the depth of our depravity and helplessness apart from God?

_____

_____

_____

_____

Day 18

Desperate for a Miracle

When she heard about Jesus, she came up behind Him in the crowd and touched His cloak, because she thought, "If I just touch His clothes, I will be healed."
Mark 5:27-28

Mark didn't mention her name. We only know that she had a seemingly incurable disease. The nonstop bleeding she experienced would have likely made her anemic and exhausted. It also made her socially unacceptable and ceremonially unclean according to Jewish Law (Leviticus 15:25-27). Consequently, marriage and childbearing would have been next to impossible. Family and friends would have been required to stay away from her. She also wouldn't have been allowed to enter the temple, thus isolating her from the faith community and preventing her from being able to worship God publicly. And on top of these challenges, she had drained all of her financial resources in an effort to find a solution to her problem.

So she took desperate measures. Risking public humiliation and possibly even punishment, she reached out to touch Jesus as He passed by in the crowd. She simply believed that He could heal her. She'd seen or heard Him do it before. And God did for her in an instant what no doctor had been able to do in twelve years.

God is moved to action when we come to Him in faith and desperation as our best and only hope. You won't automatically be healed of every health problem or see a breakthrough in every circumstance just by having faith, but you will be transformed from the inside out and you will experience the peace of God like never before.

Your Personal Reflection and Application

If you read the entire account (Mark 5:24-34) you'll see that Jesus made the woman reveal herself. Why do you think He did that?

_____

_____

_____

_____

Why would God allow this woman to suffer for twelve years when He could have healed her from the beginning?

_____

_____

_____

_____

_____

Have you ever been in such a dire situation that you felt like God was your only hope? What did that circumstance teach you about faith and about God?

_____

_____

_____

_____

_____

Day 19

Between a Rock and a Hard Place

"Do not be afraid. Stand firm and you will see the deliverance the Lord will bring you today. The Egyptians you see today you will never see again. The Lord will fight for you; you need only to be still."
Exodus 14:13-14

It's difficult to imagine a more desperate situation than the one in which the Israelites found themselves in Exodus 14. The Red Sea prevented them from being able to move forward. At the same time, the mighty Egyptian army – from whom the Israelites had just miraculously escaped after having endured 400 years of oppressive enslavement in Egypt – were now chasing after Israel and about to overtake them from behind.

Surrounded on all sides with no escape in sight, the Israelites were understandably terrified. So, Israel initially did what many of us do when we're caught in a desperate circumstance: they grumbled and complained to God (vv. 8-12).

God, however, supernaturally brought about Israel's deliverance by parting the waters of the Red Sea, allowing the Israelites to pass through safely, while the Egyptian army drowned (vv. 21-29).

Why does God allow us to go through seemingly impossible circumstances like these? Often it's because He wants to get our attention. He wants our devotion. He wants our *desperation.* He wants us to learn to trust Him above anything or anyone else and to call out to Him in our time of need. Perhaps He's even placed you in a desperate situation right now so that He will be your only solution, so that you will be still, stop relying on your own timing and resources, and witness just how powerful and sufficient He is.

Your Personal Reflection and Application

Can you identify with the Israelites in this story? If so, how?

_____

_____

_____

What might it mean to "stand firm" and to "be still" (vv. 13-14) when you're in a desperate circumstance?

_____

_____

_____

How does God "fight" for us (v. 14)?

_____

_____

_____

When the Israelites got to the other side of the Red Sea and realized the miraculous breakthrough that had just taken place, they gave thanks to God and worshiped Him (Exodus 15). Take a moment to tell God thank you for the times that He has been faithful and delivered you out of difficult circumstances.

_____

_____

_____

Day 20

Hungry for God

"As the deer pants for streams of water,
so my soul pants for You, my God."
Psalm 42:1

It's one thing to pray for God to come through for you when you're in a desperate situation and need a miracle. It's another thing, however, to be desperately hungry *for God Himself.*

Psalm 42 illustrates that spiritual desperation isn't so much about wanting God to "show up" and to change your circumstances, as it is about already having a vibrant relationship with God – and longing for *more* of it. Spiritual desperation is about more than asking God to change your situation. It's about asking God to actually change *you.* It's about putting your total and complete hope in Him (vv. 5, 11), not in your own wisdom or strength. It's about yearning and aching to know God more, to hear Him speak to you, and to personally feel His presence and witness His power in a fresh way.

Take a few minutes to read through Psalm 42.

Would you describe yourself as someone who is desperate for more of God? If not, what's holding you back?

Let's admit it. Most of us are not as hungry or as thirsty for God as we should be. But one of the great promises in the Bible is that God draws near to those who draw near to Him (James 4:8). Like the psalmist, express your utter dependence upon God in prayer and your earnest desire to know Him more today.

Your Personal Reflection and Application

What specific words or phrases do you see in Psalm 42 that describe the psalmist's hunger for God?

_____

_____

_____

_____

What is the difference between wanting something from God and wanting God Himself?

_____

_____

_____

_____

_____

Take a moment and ask God to show you anything that is getting in the way of you being more desperate for Him. Write down anything that He lays on your heart.

_____

_____

_____

_____

_____

Day 21

Application Day: Silence & Stillness

It can be challenging to find silence and solitude in our lives. Even when we sit down or lay in bed, our minds tend to stay active. It seems every part of our day is inundated with noise and activity. And one of the times in our lives when our minds and hearts tend to race the most is during seasons of desperation. When we're desperate, we get anxious and it's difficult for us to be still. We can easily spend way too much time worrying and thinking about solutions to the problems we face. And when that happens, we can miss hearing God speak to us.

Take time today to be silent and still before God. It may feel completely counterintuitive and counterproductive to do so. You may even feel it's a waste of time. And yet, in quietness you can often notice things and hear words from God you would normally not notice, hear, or feel.

So be still, and know that God alone is God (Psalm 46:10). Cease from striving and be alone with Him for part of the day. Here are some ideas to help you get started:

- If silence is new for you, start with 10-15 minutes. You can even set a timer to keep you from watching the clock. Just remember that it can take a few minutes to quiet your spirit and to shut off your active mind and any noise around you.

- Start your time by telling God, "Here I am, Lord. Speak to me, and I will listen."

- Taking some deep breaths and relaxing your body will help you to slow down.

- Lastly, keep in mind that the purpose of this exercise is not simply to be silent, but to open yourself to being present before God.

Week 4

Fervent

Therefore confess your sins to each other and pray for each other so that you may be healed. The prayer of a righteous man is powerful and effective.

James 5:16

Day 22: Introduction to Week 4

All of us can relate to going through seasons in which our passion or enthusiasm for doing certain activities decreases. Sometimes we simply lose interest over time. We get busy doing other things. We encounter some type of crisis or resistance that shakes our confidence. We discover that it's harder than we expected to finish what we've started. We begin to question if it's worth the time and energy we're investing. We lose heart.

The same thing can happen in our prayer lives. If we're not careful, we can easily lose our passion and our motivation and, before we know it, we either stop praying altogether or begin falling into patterns of shallow, formulaic, watered-down prayers in which we hastily come before God and spend the bulk of our prayer time mindlessly and superficially running through a list of things we'd like Him to do in our lives.

God doesn't ever want you to forget who you're talking to in prayer. Nor does He want you to be satisfied with a mediocre or half-hearted prayer life. He wants you to earnestly seek Him in prayer with zeal and with your *whole* heart (Jeremiah 29:12-13). He wants a vibrant relationship with you and He wants to use prayer as a means for you to know Him more. He wants to bring you to deeper levels of dependence on Him.

So, are you open to having God do whatever it takes to give you a renewed sense of passion and urgency in your prayer life? If you are, then ask Him to do just that this week.

Watch Video 4   Fervent

Your notes:

_____

_____

_____

What can we learn about fervent prayer from Daniel?

1. Fervent prayer was _____ in Daniel's life.

2. Fervent prayer is _____ whenever we are immersed in God's Word.

3. Fervent prayer is _____.

4. Fervent prayer _____ God's interests and His glory.

Personal Response:

1. What did you hear?

_____

_____

2. How do you hope to respond?

_____

_____

Questions for Group Discussion

1. Who is someone whose prayer life you admire? Why?

2. Read Daniel 9:1-19 in order to better observe the various elements of his prayer. What initial things stand out to you?

3. How does prayer that arises from reading God's Word add energy and sincerity to our prayers?

4. How is Daniel's prayer similar in pattern to the Lord's Prayer (Luke 11:2-4)?

5. Why is it significant that Daniel prayed with fasting and in sackcloth and ashes (v. 3)?

6. What role should adoration for God play in our prayers? What words or phrases does Daniel use to express his adoration for God?

7. What role should confession and repentance from sin play in our prayers? What does the fact that confession follows adoration teach us? What words or phrases does Daniel use as part of his time of confession?

8. Would you say that your prayers are primarily motivated by God's glory and His interests? Why or why not? Why is this an important consideration when it comes to praying with greater fervency?

9. Why does God care about whether or not our prayers are heartfelt?

Week 4

Personal Daily Devotions

Fervent

Therefore confess your sins to each other and pray for each other so that you may be healed. The prayer of a righteous man is powerful and effective.

James 5:16

Day 23

What is Fervent Prayer?

"The effective, fervent prayer of a righteous man avails much."
James 5:16b (NKJV)

While we should always check to make sure that our prayers are in line with God's will (1 John 5:14-15) and that we are praying with the right motives (James 4:3), today's theme verse indicates that God mercifully and mightily responds when His children offer up fervent prayers.

What, then, is *fervent* praying? And is it possible that we are not as fervent in our praying as we should be?

The specific Greek word that James uses in v. 16 for *fervent* describes having intense feeling or enthusiasm for something. Elsewhere in the New Testament another word for *fervent* is sometimes used which means "to boil" or "to be hot." To pray with fervency, then, is to pray from the heart with great intensity, urgency, and energy. It's to pray with determination regardless of how much Satan tries to discourage you. And as we'll see this week, fervent prayers very often mean taking action.

Fervency in prayer is not about being longwinded or superficially emotional. Fervent prayers are sincere. They are reliable indicators of your priorities, motives, and the condition of your heart before God.

So, if you find you've recently been lacking in fervor, start by reminding yourself of the incredible privilege you have in prayer. Prayer is not some incantation or magic formula, but it is a powerful means of communication with the Creator and Sustainer of the universe. Ask Him today for the zeal and boldness in prayer that He wants you to have.

Your Personal Reflection and Application

How does today's verse encourage or challenge you?

_____

_____

_____

_____

_____

What does your current degree of fervency in prayer say about what you believe to be true about prayer? About God?

_____

_____

_____

_____

_____

How might last week's topic of desperation for God and this week's topic of fervency in prayer be connected?

_____

_____

_____

_____

_____

Day 24

Fervent Prayer in Action

"Elijah was a human being, even as we are. He prayed earnestly that it would not rain, and it did not rain on the land for three and a half years. Again he prayed, and the heavens gave rain, and the earth produced its crops."
James 5:17-18

To illustrate how the fervent prayers of God's children accomplish much (James 5:16b), the book of James points us to the prayer life of the prophet Elijah.

Like us, Elijah was a normal, sinful human being. Nevertheless, we read in 1 Kings 17 that he prayed earnestly that it would not rain on the land so that Ahab, the wicked king of Israel, would humble himself before God. And in answer to Elijah's fervent prayer, God caused it to not rain for three and a half years. 1 Kings 18 then tells us that, after the people of Israel finally turned to God in desperation, Elijah prayed once again. In response, God produced a heavy rainstorm.

Notice the earnestness and zeal with which Elijah prayed. He "bent down to the ground and put his face between his knees" (1 Kings 18:42). And as he waited for the rain to come, he persisted in prayer, even to the point of ordering his servant seven different times to report back on how God was answering his prayers (vv. 43-45).

Do you believe that God can bring about a breakthrough in your circumstances? Consider the influence one ordinary individual can have when they passionately and urgently come before an extraordinary God in prayer!

Your Personal Reflection and Application

What does Elijah's physical posture in prayer indicate about the posture of his heart toward God? Why is this important?

_____

_____

_____

_____

What point might James be trying to make in v. 17 when he says that "Elijah was a human being, even as we are"?

_____

_____

_____

_____

Has God ever stirred within your heart a desire to pray for something so enormous that only He could make it happen? What did that experience teach you?

_____

_____

_____

_____

Day 25

An Earnest Plea for a Prisoner

*"So Peter was kept in prison, but the church
was earnestly praying to God for him."*
Acts 12:5

The apostle Peter was asleep in prison. Having been placed there by King Herod for spreading the good news of Jesus Christ, Peter awaited his trial the following day, at which time he would likely be sentenced to death. To prevent Peter from escaping, Herod assigned four squads of soldiers to guard him. The situation appeared hopeless.

In response, the Christian church prayed together throughout the night – *earnestly*.

Picture a rope that is fully stretched out, pulled tight, without any slack. Or picture a hand that is extended and desperately grasping for something. That is actually what the Greek word for *earnestly* means in Acts 12:5. The same root word is used in Luke 22:44 when it says that Jesus prayed "more earnestly" in the Garden of Gethsemane and, in agony, actually sweat drops of blood.

The idea that Luke, the author of Acts, is conveying is that the church was not simply running through a casual listing of prayer requests. They were fervently and strenuously praying to God for Peter with all of the passion and energy they could corporately muster.

As a result of their earnest prayers, God broke through and did the unthinkable, rescuing and releasing Peter from prison.

Never doubt the power of prayer. Prayer is not a last option – something to turn to when all else fails or you've explored every other possible option. It is the first, best, and most powerful thing you can ever do.

Your Personal Reflection and Application

While God can respond to the prayer of just one person, today's story also illustrates the power of corporate prayer. It's an encouragement whenever we're willing to share prayer burdens with other believers. How might praying for a particular need with others stimulate you to pray with greater fervor and faith? When have you witnessed God do something miraculous in response to corporate prayer?

_____

_____

_____

_____

_____

Think of some Christ-followers who are currently undergoing persecution for the sake of the gospel. (If you need some ideas, a quick internet search may be helpful.) List their names below, and spend some time today interceding on their behalf. Pray that the message of the gospel would spread as a result of, or in spite of, this persecution.

_____

_____

_____

_____

_____

Day 26

Fasting for a Breakthrough

"But when you fast, put oil on your head and wash your face,
so that it will not be obvious to others that you are fasting,
but only to your Father, who is unseen; and your Father,
who sees what is done in secret, will reward you."
Matthew 6:17-18

If you are sincerely interested in growing in zeal for God and praying with greater levels of desperation and fervor than ever before, one of the best – and also one of the most neglected – practices you can undertake is the discipline of fasting.

Fasting – intentionally and temporarily forgoing a normal necessity or routine in order to devote yourself to prayer and to drawing closer to God – has been practiced for millennia by Old Testament saints on down to the present day. It is often done when making important decisions (Acts 13:2; 14:23), to express repentance (2 Samuel 12:16) or humility (Psalm 35:13-14), when embarking upon a new season of life or ministry (Matthew 4:1-2), or to simply demonstrate your dependence upon God.

Jesus' statement above (*"when* you fast") indicates that fasting is normal, acceptable, and expected in the Christian life. And yet, many people never consider fasting when they're praying for a breakthrough. We don't think we can go without food (or caffeine, media, technology, or whatever it is that you normally depend upon). But that's precisely the point. Fasting is putting your fervor into action. It is saying to God, "Lord, you are more important to me than _____. I long to hear from You, so take my eyes off of the things of this world in order to focus more completely on You."

Your Personal Reflection and Application

What is your attitude toward fasting or self-denial? What are your concerns?

_____

_____

_____

_____

Should fasting be considered as a way to manipulate God to do what you want or as a way to demonstrate that you are more spiritual than others? Why or why not?

_____

_____

_____

_____

_____

What kind of "rewards" from fasting might Jesus be referring to in today's Scripture passage?

_____

_____

_____

_____

_____

Day 27

Praying the Scriptures

"Oh, how I love Your law! I meditate on it all day long."
Psalm 119:97

How should you pray when you don't know what to pray? How can you keep your prayers from becoming stale or monotonous?

Hopefully this week's devotionals have been helpful in addressing some of those concerns. One further action step to consider making a regular practice, though, is to pray Scripture back to God. The early church prayed the Scriptures (Acts 4:23-31). Many parts of Scripture – especially the book of Psalms – are, in fact, ready-made prayers (e.g., Psalm 63; Matthew 6:9-13; Ephesians 3:14-21). Bible verses are a great means for praying more earnestly and fervently, because they can focus your mind on what matters most and ensure that you are praying in accordance with God's will (1 John 5:14).

Start by using a verse or a passage to shape your prayer. Simply pray the verse or passage back to God. Personalize it by substituting in your name or the name of someone for whom you are interceding. Use verses to cry for help to God or to give thanks to Him because of who Scripture reveals Him to be.

As with fasting or praying in general, your focus should always be on God first, rather than viewing prayer as some type of formula to get God to give you what you want. Prayer is less about how and what you say, and more about fervently drawing near to the merciful, miracle-working God to whom you are praying.

Your Personal Reflection and Application

What prayers of the Bible have helped you in the past?

_____

_____

_____

_____

_____

How might praying Scripture add new life and fervency to how you normally approach prayer?

_____

_____

_____

_____

_____

As you reflect back upon this week's devotionals and teaching on fervent prayer, what specifically has God revealed to you? What are some next steps you need to begin taking?

_____

_____

_____

_____

_____

Days 28

Application Day: Fasting

"Is not this the kind of fasting I have chosen: to loose the chains of injustice and untie the cords of the yoke, to set the oppressed free and break every yoke?"
Isaiah 58:6

We took a brief look this week at the discipline of fasting, particularly as it pertains to fervent prayer. You don't have to have previous experience with fasting in order to benefit from it. It is a meaningful way to express your devotion to God and to seek God's will and grace beyond your normal habits of prayer and worship.

With this in mind, prayerfully consider an appetite (e.g., a meal, media, technology) from which you can abstain for part or all of today. Here are some suggestions to get the most out of this exercise:

- Pray for wisdom (James 1:5) about what God would want you to abstain from today in order to more fully attend to Him in prayer.

- If you decide to fast from a meal, be sure to stay hydrated.

- You should consider postponing your fast if you are sick or in a hurry today. It's important to be able to give God your full attention during the fast.

- If you are new to fasting and aren't sure how to start, simply spend the time with God in prayer and in Scripture that you would normally spend on whatever activity it is from which you are abstaining. When your stomach growls or you are tempted to give in to your appetite, use that as an opportunity to express your desire for God to speak to and sustain you.

- Keep in mind that the Enemy will try to discourage or dissuade you from fasting. Expect temptation or discouragement.

- Be mindful of your motivations. The point of fasting is not to focus on yourself, but to focus on God.

Write down any insights God gives you during your fast. You may not necessarily see or sense any immediate "fruit" from your fast, but offer your desires and prayers to God in faith and as a sacrifice of praise.

Week 5

Persistent

Let us not become weary in doing good, for at the proper time we will reap a harvest if we do not give up.

Galatians 6:9

Day 29: Introduction to Week 5

To give up or to keep going? Often both paths seem like terrible options. Both hurt. Neither appear like they will get us what we want. Yet, we need to do *something*. Choosing not to act at all is choosing to give up. So, what should we do? What does God want us to do?

When it comes to prayer, what does God want us to do when nothing seems to be happening in response to our prayers? When we are waiting on that breakthrough, what do we do? Give up? Keep praying?

If we're honest, there is only one logical answer. If we give up, there is no hope. If we keep praying, even though it might seem impossible, at least there is a chance. As long as we are still moving, grasping, asking, the breakthrough could come.

God wants us to be persistent in our prayers. He doesn't want us to give up. And the good news is that He doesn't leave us alone in this struggle to persist. We are given all the help we need to keep going. To keep trusting. To keep praying.

Watch Video 5   **Persistent**

Your notes:

_____

_____

_____

_____

1. God asks us to pray _____ and works

    in _____ to persistent prayer.

2. The _____ of persistent prayer is just as

    important as the _____.

3. Through persistence, God will lead us to the

    _____ that we need.

Questions for Group Discussion

---

1. Could you relate to any of the examples given in the video?

2. What biblical examples of persistent prayer come to mind?

3. Have you ever persisted in prayer for a long time until God answered? What happened? What door opened? Was it what you expected?

4. Has there been a time in your life when you decided to stop praying? What happened?

5. For what are you persisting now?

Week 5

Personal Daily Devotions

Persistent

Let us not become weary in doing good, for at the proper time we will reap a harvest if we do not give up.

Galatians 6:9

Day 30

God's persistence precedes ours

*"....He who began a good work in you will carry it
on to completion until the day of Christ Jesus."*
Philippians 1:6

Sometimes we want to give up persistently praying for a breakthrough because we believe the outcome is simply out of reach. We think, "I've been praying about this for a long time and nothing has happened." Our loved one will never come to know Christ, or we will never get *that* job even though we are more than qualified, or we will never have the relationship or marriage that others seem to have, or our church will never see masses of people give their lives to Christ.

So why keep at it?

One reason is because God never gives up on us. He has promised to complete the work He began in us which, if we are willing to admit it, is quite the task! God has every reason to write us off, and yet He has decided to stand with us to the end.

Whatever we are facing is not as difficult as God's work in us to turn us from sinners to saints. Since He has committed Himself to that work, why not commit ourselves to His work through our prayers? We trust Him to bring us safely to moralistic perfection in eternity even though there are many days that could make us believe we will never make it. Why not also trust Him to bring about the best possible outcome in all other circumstances?

Wherever you have given up hope, turn to God and talk with Him about it now. Even if you've brought it before him a million times in the past, bring it to Him again. And again. He has never given up on you, so don't give up on Him.

Your Personal Reflection and Application

If God has never and will never give up on you, what reason could you have to give up on your prayers to Him?

_____

_____

_____

_____

Is there anything you believe to be more seemingly impossible than your transformation from sinner to saint? Are you trusting that God will definitely complete that work?

_____

_____

_____

_____

Are there any specific prayers that you have given up praying because you haven't seen God answering? Write them out below and lift them up to God again.

_____

_____

_____

_____

_____

Day 31

God's persistence joins ours

"But if we hope for what we do not yet have, we wait for it patiently. In the same way, the Spirit helps us in our weakness. We do not know what we ought to pray for, but the Spirit Himself intercedes for us through wordless groans."

Romans 8:25-26

Sometimes all it takes to make it through a struggle is to know that we are not alone. Having someone in the trenches with us can change even the direst of circumstances into bearable ones. Children instinctively grab the hand of a parent when they are scared because they don't want to face the fear alone, and they believe the parent will know what to do.

As Christians, God never leaves us alone. He is in every trench, every circumstance, and every fear praying with us. Even when we aren't praying, He is. Even when we don't feel like we have the strength to pray for that breakthrough one more time, God never falters.

Seeing His persistence can help our own. Knowing He is laboring in prayer with us can give us the strength to carry on ourselves. When this passage describes how God's Spirit groans for us, it does not depict a passing concern for our welfare. God feels our pains, our hopes, and our longings perhaps even more deeply than we do, and His response is prayer.

Since we have such a faithful Father who holds our hand through every battle, binding Himself to us in prayer, let us continue to cling to Him even if all we can muster are the same wordless groans.

Your Personal Reflection and Application

When are the times you typically feel like giving up in prayer?

_____

_____

_____

_____

_____

On whom can you most depend to pray for you when you are in the middle of one of those times?

_____

_____

_____

_____

_____

If God Himself has promised to pray for you, have you ever asked Him to pray for you like you'd ask a friend to pray for you? Have you ever thanked Him for praying for you?

_____

_____

_____

_____

_____

Day 32

Peace after struggle

"My soul is overwhelmed with sorrow to the point of death," He said to them. "Stay here and keep watch." Going a little farther, He fell to the ground and prayed that if possible the hour might pass from Him. "Abba, Father," He said, "everything is possible for You. Take this cup from Me. Yet not what I will, but what You will."
Mark 14:34-36

This is one moment when it seems like even Jesus didn't have peace. He knew (better than we will ever understand) how it would feel to pay for the sin of the world on the cross, and the thought of it was tearing Him apart.

So what did He do?

He prayed. When Jesus was struggling with matters as deep as heaven and hell, eternal separation, and atonement for the sum total of all evil, He went to the Father. He pleaded His case, and He listened for God's response.

When He began praying, He was wrapped in turmoil, but by the time He finished, He had peace. Even though the exact same set of events would still unfold, now He had peace.

This is what persistence in prayer will always produce. Peace. The circumstances may not change, but if we wrestle with God long enough, He will calm the storm of our hearts. God invites us to yell and argue, to be angry and desperate, and even to pitch a fit.

But He wants us to do it all with Him in prayer. As He invites us into that type of raw relationship, He wants us to invite Him into the same. He says, "Give me your real thoughts, but let me give you mine as well." When we listen long enough to hear His voice, we find peace.

Your Personal Reflection and Application

How raw have you been with God? Have you ever told Him that you are angry? Have you ever told Him that you don't know how to trust Him?

_____

_____

_____

_____

_____

_____

How can you invite God to be that raw with you? Is there anything "off limits" that you don't want God to tell you? Is there anything He could ask you to do that you would say no?

_____

_____

_____

_____

_____

_____

_____

Day 33

Strength After Waiting

"Even youths shall faint and be weary, and young men shall fall exhausted, but they who wait for the Lord shall renew their strength; they shall mount up with wings like eagles; they shall run and not be weary; they shall walk and not faint."   –Isaiah 40:30-31

There is no way to have persistence in prayer unless we are waiting. There would be no reason for it. Only when we wait do we need persistence.

But oh how we hate to wait! Days extend to weeks, which drag into months, which form into years, and yet, we still wait. From our perspective, it doesn't seem like we should need to wait because other people aren't waiting. Other people seem to get exactly what they want the moment they want it. More frustrating is when we see other people get exactly what *we* want without much waiting at all.

Why them? Why not us? Why not now?

Isaiah tells us. Those who wait upon the Lord will renew their strength. God makes us wait in order to give us strength. While we can sometimes believe this verse promises the outcome we desire, it does not. It only makes one promise – strength to those who wait. More specifically, it promises strength to those who *wait on the Lord*. Strength may not come if we are simply waiting for our desired outcome.

But for those of us who want the Lord more than we want the chips to fall in our favor, strength is on its way. There are times when God withholds what we want in order to change us into the type of people who only want Him. When He achieves that in us, only then can we run without growing weary and walk without becoming faint.

Your Personal Reflection and Application

For what are you currently waiting? Is it for the Lord to answer in His way and His time? Or something else?

_____

_____

_____

_____

What do you find is the hardest part about waiting? Not having what you want? Not knowing if you will get what you want? Seeing others have what you want? Something else?

_____

_____

_____

_____

Do you believe it is worth it for God to postpone His answer in order that you may find Him in a deeper and fuller way?

_____

_____

_____

_____

Day 34

Response After Crying

"And will not God bring about justice for His chosen ones, who cry out to him day and night? Will He keep putting them off?"

Luke 18:7

God will break through. Why He lingers can certainly confuse and frustrate us at times, but what He has promised will come to pass. Justice for those who cry out to Him – who continue to cry out to Him in persistence.

Where do you see that our world is wrong? Where do you see that our church is wrong? Where do you see that your family and group of friends is wrong? Where do you see that you are wrong?

Have you stopped crying out to God about it? It's time to start again. God waits for appointed times, but He also waits for our prayers. He tells us we *have* not because we *ask* not.

In the end, He will wrap up the sky like a scroll, wipe every tear from every eye, and execute perfect justice upon all of history. Everything that has been wrong will be set right.

If we know this is what God has planned, let us join with Him in bringing it about through our prayers.

"Lord, come quickly, and do not delay. Thy will be done on earth as it is in heaven. May Your justice come and be a light to the nations, and may Your righteousness draw speedily near as we wait in hope of Your salvation."

Your Personal Reflection and Application

For what do you cry out for day and night?

_____

_____

_____

_____

_____

_____

_____

If you aren't currently crying out day and night, what would make you pray like that? What do you see that is horribly wrong in the world, in our church, in your family, or in yourself?

_____

_____

_____

_____

_____

_____

_____

Day 35

Application Day: Reminder Needed?

Persistence takes more than one day. Think of Ralphie in the movie *A Christmas Story*, who worked and worked and worked to convince his parents or Santa or anyone to give him a BB gun for Christmas. His persistence took many forms and was spread out over a long period of time.

So while we can begin persistence today, we won't come anywhere near to accomplishing it in just a day or two.

They say it takes weeks to develop a new habit. While the exact number of days is a bit hazy and differs from person to person, we know it takes longer than we would like – meaning we are going to need some reminders to keep going.

Over the course of this last week, God has probably prompted you to pray more frequently for some specific things. If you have a phone, take it out and set a daily, weekly, or bi-weekly reminder to pray. When your reminder alerts you, take a moment to pray for those specific things. Plan to do this for at least a year or until you receive God's answer.

If you aren't familiar with setting a reminder on your phone, have someone help you do it. Or you can create a prayer event for yourself on a website like Evite that will automatically send reminders to you through email. Or you can break out your pencil and put a post-it by your toothbrush or schedule meetings with God in the calendar you use, in order to pray through the next year.

Whatever you do to remind yourself, take these appointments seriously. If you miss one, be sure to reschedule it the same as you would reschedule any other vitally critical meeting.

Week 6

Expectant

Give ear to my words, O LORD, consider my sighing. Listen to my cry for help, my King and my God, for to You I pray. In the morning, O LORD, You hear my voice; in the morning I lay my requests before You and wait in expectation.

Psalm 5:1-3

Day 36: Introduction to Week 6

As we come to the last few days in our *Only by Prayer* series, let's take a quick look back. Over the past thirty-five days we've seen:

1. Prayers that break through are RELIANT

2. Prayers that break through are REPENTANT

3. Prayers that break through are DESPERATE

4. Prayers that break through are FERVENT

5. Prayers that break through are PERSISTENT

Now as we bring our series to a close, we will focus on this final essential matter:

6. Prayers that break through are EXPECTANT

Jesus prayed with expectant belief. He knew God heard His prayers and He expected God to act in accordance with His divine plan and will. That was evident when Jesus, before calling Lazarus out of the tomb, looked up to Heaven and prayed:

> *Father, I thank You that You have heard me. I know that You always hear me, but I said this for the benefit of the people standing here, that they may believe that You sent me* (John 11:41).

Like Jesus prayed with expectant belief, He wants the same from His followers. He wants us to come to Him with the same attitude Mary and her sister Martha had when they sent word to Jesus that their brother Lazarus was sick.

Lazarus' sisters believed that Jesus wanted His followers to come to Him in their times of need. And that's exactly what they did. They sent word to Jesus that their brother was sick, because they believed that Jesus, who loved them and their brother, would come to his side and heal him.

You might think that when Jesus got the message that Lazarus was gravely ill, He would have rushed to him like a paramedic unit with lights flashing and siren blaring. But he didn't. *"Jesus loved Martha and her sister and Lazarus. Yet when he heard that Lazarus was sick, he stayed where he was two more days"* (John 11:5-6).

From our perspective, that seems like an odd way to show someone love in a time of desperate need. Jesus seemingly did nothing for two days and then made the trip to Bethany and arrived *after* Lazarus had already been dead and buried in a tomb for four days (John 11:39).

Put yourself in Martha and Mary's shoes. They believed their brother would not have died if Jesus had been there before he died. Each of them was so certain of that fact, that they – independent of the other – told Jesus, *"If You had been here, my brother would not have died"* (John 11:22,32).

They knew Jesus could have prevented their brother's death, so they were confused. Their grief-filled words said it all. "Lord, why didn't You come?"

Jesus could have come *before* Lazarus died. But he didn't. For a good reason. He wanted His followers to learn a life-lesson about expectant belief. The kind of belief that Jesus lived with, and prayed with. The kind of expectant prayer that can even bring life after death.

Watch Video 6   **Expectant**

Your notes:

_____

_____

_____

_____

Expectant prayer:

1. Knows God _____

    John 11:41-42 – Then Jesus looked up and said, "*Father, I thank You that You have heard me. I knew that You always hear me, but I said this for the benefit of the people standing here, that they may believe that You sent me.*"

2. Believes God _____

    John 11:42b – "*that they may believe that You sent me.*"

3. Seeks God's _____

    John 11:40 – Then Jesus said, "Did I not tell you that if you believed, you would see the glory of God?"

Questions for Group Discussion

1. Prior to today, what different things have you heard people say about expectant belief as it relates to prayer?

2. Can you think of a time in your life when you came to the Lord and it seemed like He ignored your prayers? How did you deal with how you felt?

3. Have you come to believe God actually hears your prayers? If so, when? In what ways has that belief changed your prayer life?

4. When Martha objected to Jesus' "*take away the stone*" command (John 11:38), Jesus countered with the question, "*Did I not tell you that if you believed, you would see the glory of God?*" Why is belief connected to seeing God's glory?

5. When Lazarus was raised from the dead, God's glory was in full display. When God answers prayer today, are His answers still for His glory? How should knowing this change the focus of how and why we pray?

6. Expectant belief is willing to wait on God's timing and trust God's plan, for God's glory. In what ways can the Lazarus story help you pray and live with both in full focus?

Week 6

Personal Daily Devotions

Expectant

Give ear to my words, O LORD, consider my sighing. Listen to my cry for help, my King and my God, for to You I pray. In the morning, O LORD, You hear my voice; in the morning I lay my requests before You and wait in expectation.

Psalm 5:1-3

Day 37

Expectant prayer asks for God's help

You do not have, because you do not ask God.
James 4:2b

God is ready to answer your prayers, if you ask. In the words of John Piper, "God ordains to fulfill His plans by being asked to do so by us."

Really? God wants me to ask for His help and even waits for me to ask before He helps? Yes, that's exactly what the Bible teaches.

> *Matthew 7:7-8,11 – "Ask and it will be given to you; seek and you will find; knock and the door will be opened to you. For everyone who asks receives; he who seeks finds; and to him who knocks, the door will be opened.* If you, then, though you are evil, know how to give good gifts to your children, how much more will your Father in heaven give good gifts to those who ask Him!

> *John 14:13 – "And I will do whatever you ask in my name, so that the Son may bring glory to the Father."*

> *John 16:24 – "Until now you have not asked for anything in my name. Ask and you will receive, and your joy will be complete."*

> *James 1:5 – If any of you lacks wisdom, he should ask God, who gives generously to all without finding fault, and it will be given to him.*

God wants us to ask for His help. He wants us to want His help. He wants us to acknowledge our need for His help. He wants us to readily seek His help, like a child seeks a parent's help.

Do you remember asking your parents for help? "Dad, can you help me tie my shoes?" "Mom, can you help me with my homework?" Why did you ask for help? Because you needed it and you knew they could help. The fact is, you still need help. And your heavenly Father is ready to give it, if you will just ask.

Your Personal Reflection and Application

Do you believe that God is able and willing to help you in your times of need?

_____

_____

_____

Are you a person who seeks God's help readily or reluctantly? What does your answer tell you about yourself?

_____

_____

_____

Where do you need God's help today? Have you asked Him for His help? Taking into account our *Only by Prayer* focus to date, in what ways have you asked for help?

_____

_____

_____

Billy Graham used to say, "Heaven is full of answers to prayer for which no one ever bothered to ask." How does this possibility impact you?

_____

_____

_____

Day 38

Expectant prayer asks with faith

But when you ask, you must believe and not doubt, because the one who doubts is like a wave of the sea... That man should not expect to receive anything from the Lord. —James 1:6-7

There is a right and a wrong way to ask for help. That's an important learning for a kid. If you need your parents' help, don't ask for it in a demanding, whining, disrespectful way. Your attitude when asking matters. As does the timing. If you just brought home a bad grade on your report card, the moment your parents see the grade is not the best time to ask for a raise in your allowance or a later curfew.

There is also a right and wrong way to ask for God's help. How you ask will impact the outcome.

The right way to ask God for help is with belief – with expectant faith. You must come to God believing that He wants you to ask; that He hears you when you ask; that He is capable of doing what is humanly impossible due to His omnipotent power; that He delights in giving good things to those who ask.

Expectant prayer believes that God's will is best. Like Jesus, it prays, *"Father, all things are possible for You.... Yet not what I will, but what You will"* (Mark 14:36). When you pray in this way, with godly motives (James 4:3) and according to God's will (1 John 5:14), you can be sure God will answer your prayers. You can believe that you will receive an answer according to God's riches in glory in Christ Jesus (Philippians 4:19).

Yes, there is a right way to ask for God's help. Come to God with belief in His goodness and power and perfect will. Not demanding your will be done, but trusting in God to do what is best.

Your Personal Reflection and Application

Recall a time in your life when you asked for something from someone and your request was not granted.

_____

_____

When you ask for God's help, do you seek to relinquish your will for God's? Do you want God to do what He deems best or what you think is best?

_____

_____

_____

Can you think of times when you've asked for God's help and things did not go as you thought they should? In looking back, why do you think He didn't answer the way you wanted Him to?

_____

_____

_____

Expectant prayer trusts in God – in who He is and what He chooses to do or not do. Why is this perspective vital to praying with belief?

_____

_____

_____

Day 39

Expectant prayer asks without doubt

But when you ask, you must believe and not doubt, because he who doubts is like a wave of the sea, blown and tossed by the wind. That man should not think he will receive anything from the Lord. —James 1:6-7

If your relationship with God is on and off, like an unstable dating relationship, don't expect God to overlook your doubts and give you the help you need.

Doubt is like a wave of the sea that is blown and tossed back and forth. It's up and down, unsettled and unpredictable. When it comes to ocean waters, that's expected and even enchanting. But when it comes to our relationship with God, an in and out, He loves me, He loves me not, relationship is unacceptable.

Expectant prayer that leads to God-sized breakthroughs doesn't doubt God's unending love. It knows God can be trusted. It believes the Lord's plan is perfect and His power is unlimited. That means we can KNOW beyond a shadow of doubt:

- *God loves us more than we can even understand*
- *God can be trusted*
- *God hears us when we call out to Him*
- *God will answer us*

It's this kind of undoubting, expectant faith that was behind the writer of Hebrews saying, "Let us then approach the throne of grace with confidence, so that we may receive mercy and find grace to help us in our time of need" (Hebrews 4:16).

Lay aside your doubts. Pray with expectant belief, knowing that God not only hears you, He is also able and ready to help you.

Your Personal Reflection and Application

Do you live with doubts when it comes to God answering your prayers? List them below. Can you see any common reasons for why doubts come your way?

_____

_____

_____

Why are doubts not in line with God's plan in our lives? Why might doubts stand in the way of God answering our prayers?

_____

_____

_____

What can you do to alleviate any doubts that might stand in the way of God answering your prayers?

_____

_____

_____

Write out a simple prayer confessing any doubts that you have about God and asking for His divine help in trusting Him more.

_____

_____

_____

Day 40

Expectant prayer willingly waits

*In the morning, O LORD, You hear my voice; in the morning
I lay my requests before You and wait in expectation.*
Psalm 5:3

Most of us hate to wait...for anything. Even in something as mundane and insignificant as ordering at a fast food restaurant. We get frustrated when we have to wait too long because, after all, it's a *fast* food place! We want what we want when we want it. Which is usually right now.

It's no wonder Starbucks' "order ahead" and "grab and go" option continues to grow in popularity. The convenience of getting exactly what you want, without waiting, is a big hit in our impatient, no time to wait, world.

But a world that caters to our desire to "get what we want when we want it" could stand in the way of the valuable lessons that the Lord may want us to learn by waiting. Learning to wait patiently is one of the ways God builds character in us and teaches us to trust in His plan and His timing.

When we pray and God says "wait," He always has a good reason. Even if it's only to build trust in His plan and His will. After all, God is God and we are not. He knows best. And when we by faith don't lose heart, but continue to stay strong with expectant faith, He is glorified.

Waiting patiently also changes us. It builds character. It helps us become the people that we want to be, and that God wants us to be.

Waiting is an opportunity to grow in expectant faith as we keep praying and trusting and believing, knowing that God will answer in His perfect way when the time is perfectly right.

Your Personal Reflection and Application

In what areas of your life are you waiting on God right now? How has this time of waiting impacted you?

_____

_____

_____

On a scale of 1-10 (with 10 being best), do your prayers and perspective reflect growing or declining expectant belief?

_____

_____

_____

How consistent are you in praying like David did in his time of hardship and need (read Psalm 5)? Are you faithfully taking your requests to God every day?

_____

_____

_____

What might the Lord be saying to you right now as you expectantly wait on Him? In what ways does He want you to respond right now as you pray for a breakthrough?

_____

_____

_____

Final Application: A Half day in Prayer

*"When You said, "Seek My face," my heart said
to You, "Your face, O LORD, I shall seek."*
Psalm 27:8

Often when we think about prayer, we think of it as one-dimensional – when we pray, we talk to God. That definitely has its place. God wants us to come before His throne and honestly share what is on our hearts. But prayer is more than just us talking and God listening. Prayer is meant to be two-dimensional. It's meant to be a conversation. It's a time for us to speak while God listens, and for us to listen as God speaks.

The Bible talks about seeking God's presence. Consciously coming before God in prayer. King David spoke of this when he said, "Now set your mind and heart to seek the LORD your God..." (1 Chronicles 22:19). A conscious choice is called for.

Every one of us can benefit from an extended time in God's presence to seek His face. A time to open our hearts, minds, and souls to Him, as we speak and listen. More often than not our times with God are short, often hurried, conversations. And though there is benefit in any time we spend with God, some of the most beneficial times of prayer come when we set aside time to simply be in His presence for an extended time.

So now, before you move on from this *Only by Prayer* study, we want to encourage you to plan a half day for prayer. A time when you and God can have an extended conversation alone together for at least four or five hours. Now that may sound like a long time to devote to prayer... until you try it. Most people who do this find that the time flies by and when it's over they are refreshed and amazed at how God has connected with them in powerful ways, simply because they took the time to consciously meet with Him and listen to Him.

Here are a few suggestions to help you make it happen:

Set a time and location on your calendar that will allow you to leave your regular routine behind. And plan it now before it becomes just a nice idea! Schedule a day when you can go somewhere away from your normal life and responsibilities. Away from your spouse or kids or roommates.

Come into your half day of prayer as rested as possible. Do you remember the time when Jesus invited His disciples to join Him for prayer and they spent most of the time sleeping? Don't let that happen to you. Make sure you can be fully alert to what the Lord has for you in the extended time you've planned.

Come prepared. Bring your Bible, a pen, and a notebook or journal. Wear comfortable clothes. You may also want to bring along some water and snacks.

Plan to include two key things in your day – time to speak to God and time to listen to God.

Begin with prayer. Ask for God's help and leading. Express your love to God. Confess any known sins. Give the Lord thanks for this focused time to spend in His presence. Ask Him for guidance. Express your longing for His promptings and leadings, and your willingness to follow where He leads you in your time of prayer and in the days that follow.

Read God's Word. Let the Scriptures speak into your heart and even direct your prayers. You may find much benefit in personalizing the Bible passages you read and praying them back to God. Consider reading Psalms 1,8,15,103,141. You might also read a few of your favorite Bible passages or some of the following: Joshua 1:6-9; Proverbs 3:5-6; Philippians 4:6-7; Romans 8:18-21,28,31-39; 1 Corinthians 13:4-8a; Hebrews 11:1-6.

As you speak to God, it may be helpful to write out the burdens that are on your heart. Then as you present these concerns to God, ask Him to help you divide that list into two categories:

things you can do something about, and things that you need to simply trust God with because they are out of your control.

If you're not sure what else to pray about, consider writing out and praying over areas of your life where you need God's clear leading. Here are a few questions that you may find helpful.

– *Lord, what next step do you want me to take in our relationship?*

– *Lord, what next step do you want me to take in my relationships?*

– *Lord, what next step do you want me to take in my family?*

– *Lord, what next step in education do you want me to take?*

– *Lord, what next step do you want me to take in my ministry?*

– *Lord, what next step do you want me to take in my career?*

– *Lord, what next step do you want me to take in my finances?*

– *Lord, what next step do you want me to take in my health?*

As you listen, write down whatever thoughts God puts on your heart. It may be things you can do related to the requests you presented to God that you could actually do something about. It may be simply reminders of His power and love related to the things on the list that you can't do anything about. It may be conviction of sin. It may be a prompting for a next step He wants you to take in some area of your life.

Be flexible and let God lead. You may find that God leads your half-day of prayer in ways that you didn't plan. That's not only okay, but that could be the best thing that could happen. It is a time for you to connect with God in intimate ways and to listen for whatever He wants you to hear. What comes could lead to an unexpected breakthrough. Perhaps the very breakthrough you've been praying for over the last 40 days.

Additional Resources

Resources

For Group Leaders

Thank you for being willing to step out and lead one of the *Only by Prayer* small groups. It's our hope that God will use this study, and the times you share with your group members, to see God bring about significant spiritual breakthroughs in our lives and in our church and in the world.

Here are a few things for you to keep in mind as you prepare to lead your small group:

- **Let God help you lead your group**. Be sure to pray for God's guidance before each session. He's the one who will help people see His truth and apply it to their lives.

- **Be friendly and be yourself**. Make sure everyone feels welcome and included. And remember that you don't have to have all the answers. And you don't have to be perfect. Feel free to honestly share your own struggles with the issues that will come up in the study. Your group will only take the information as deep and as personal as you take it.

- **Be prepared**. Be sure you read the introduction, watch the video, and answer the questions ahead of time.

- **When you ask a question, give people time to respond**. Don't let silence bother you. People need to have time to think before they respond.

- **If your group is fairly large, break into smaller groups for the discussion time**. This will make it easier for people to share their answers, and more people will have the opportunity to join the discussion instead of just listening to others share their opinions.

- **Follow this format for each session:**
    - Begin each session by either personally sharing the information in the introduction, or have someone read it.
    - Watch the video.
    - Discuss.
    - Close your time in prayer.

Answers

For Video Notes

Video 1 – Reliant
1. **Before** the wall was rebuilt
2. **While** the wall was rebuilt
3. **After** the wall was rebuilt

Video 2 – Repentant
1. If we avoid confession, it leads to **shame**
2. We experience **relief** and **deliverance**
3. God will **instruct, teach,** and **counsel**

Video 3 – Desperate
1. Fear
2. Pride
3. Complacency

Video 4 – Fervent
1. Fervent prayer was **prominent** in Daniel's life
2. Fervent prayer is **prompted** whenever we are...
3. Fervent prayer is **passionate**
4. Fervent prayer **prioritizes** God's interests and His glory

Video 5 – Persistent
1. God asks us to pray **persistently** and works in **response** to persistent prayer.
2. The **journey** of persistent prayer is just as important as the **outcome**.
3. Through persistence, God will lead us to the **breakthrough** that we need.

Video 6 – Expectant
1. Knows God **hears**
2. Believes God **answers**
3. Seeks God's **glory**

Weekly

Family Devotions

Dear Parents,

No two families are exactly alike, but the consistent message of the Bible is that God's plan and purpose for every family is still the same. He wants parents, grandparents, and other people of God to pass faith along to the next generation (Deuteronomy 6:4-9; Psalm 78:1-8). One of the best ways we can carry out this important calling from God within our homes is to have intentional faith conversations with our children throughout the course of the day. With that in mind, it is our earnest prayer that this particular devotional guide will be a practical resource you can use to help point your kids to the Lord.

Within these pages you'll find six devotional readings that we encourage you to go through together with your children. Each devotion corresponds to one of the six primary topics that are covered in the 40-Day *Only by Prayer* church and small-group study. You'll also find suggestions inside this guide for shared activities and discussions that were created to help you and your kids connect with each other and to engage in meaningful and productive faith conversations.

You might want to begin and close each devotional time with a short prayer. If in your conversations your child poses a question for which you don't have an answer, don't be afraid to say "I don't know" or "Let's look in the Bible" or "Let's ask another friend at church about that."

Here are some additional ideas you may want to consider:

- Strive to make the devotions as fun and inviting for your kids as possible. You can do them outdoors, while eating popcorn together, while sitting in a booth at a restaurant, in different rooms of the house, in the morning, at nighttime before bed – anytime that works for your family and promotes interaction!

- Keep it simple. If you have younger children, you should definitely consider paraphrasing or condensing the readings and discussion questions to make the concepts easier to understand and to reinforce the main idea behind each topic.

- Keep it short. These Scripture readings are designed to foster conversation, but remember that kids (and some adults as well!) have short attention spans.

- Be intentional. Families are busier now than ever, so the more intentional you are about having devotions together, the more likely they will actually take place.

May God use these devotions to center your family's focus upon God's redeeming love as expressed through the cross, inspire you to turn to God in prayer with greater boldness and faith, and enable you to make family memories together.

Week 1

Reliant

*"After Jesus had gone indoors, his disciples asked
him privately, 'Why couldn't we drive it out?'
He replied, 'This kind can come out only by prayer.'"*
Mark 9:28-29

Do you remember a time when you were little and wanted to prove that you could do something all by yourself, without anyone helping you? Showing others that you're growing up sure is a special feeling!

The Bible tells us, though, that God loves it when we ask Him for help. He wants us to always depend upon Him. That's one of the main reasons why God created prayer. Prayer is a reminder that we need God. In fact, we *all* need God's help to be the people that God made us to be. And like today's Scripture passage tells us, there are certain things that can only happen by prayer.

Do you ever need help obeying your mom or dad? Do you need help loving someone who hurts your feelings? Do you need help trusting God when you're sick or when you're scared? Do you need help when you have a tough choice to make? Absolutely! And the best person to look to for help is God. Remember that you can always rely on Him to be there for you.

Do

Look at the following statements about prayer together, and then ask each person to share which three statements they agree with most:

- It's good to pray every day.

- Talking to God is like talking to a friend.

- I never know what to pray about.

- The best place to pray is at church.

- Praying is boring.

- People use too many big words when they pray.

- I always pray whenever I'm scared or worried.

- Sometimes I forget to pray.

- I only talk to God about big things, not little things.

- I know I can talk to God about everything.

Create a basic "prayer board" together that you can use as a family during this 40-day study. Use it to write down prayer needs as they arise. Then remember to pray regularly together about the things on the board. And be sure to check off prayer requests that God has answered!

Discuss

- Share about a time when someone was not reliable or broke a promise to you. How did that make you feel? Could you trust that person in the same way afterwards?

- How does God show us that He is always reliable?

- What are some reasons why we don't pray more often?

Week 2

Repentant

*"Create in me a pure heart, O God,
and renew a steadfast spirit within me."*
Psalm 51:10

Which do you enjoy more in the game of hide-and-seek: hiding or seeking? It seems that, if given a choice, most people find it more fun to be the one who is hiding, especially if they can find such a great place to hide that the person looking for them never finds them!

Do you know who the first people to ever play hide-and-seek were? Believe it or not, it was actually Adam and Eve. The Bible teaches us that they were so ashamed when they chose to sin against God that they actually tried hiding from Him in the Garden of Eden (Genesis 3:8). And then they tried to cover up their sin by making excuses to God (Genesis 3:12-13). As a result, their relationship with God was broken.

The truth is that we all do the same thing that Adam and Eve did. We all disobey God in various ways (Romans 3:23), and we often try to hide our sins from God. We like to pretend that they don't exist or that our sins are not that big of a deal. But they *are* a big deal, because our sins – even the little ones – separate us from God, and there is no amount of good things we can do that can change that fact (Romans 6:23).

The best news of all, though, is that Jesus died for our sins on the cross, so God makes it possible for us to be forgiven whenever we disobey Him. You don't need to hide from Him. You simply need to confess your sins to God, and He promises to forgive you and give you a clean heart (1 John 1:9).

Do

Pick an object and have family members take turns hiding the object in a room somewhere. Then have the rest of the family try to find the object. Talk afterwards about how Adam & Eve tried hiding from God.

Take a tube of toothpaste and squeeze some out on a plate or napkin. Then try to put the toothpaste back into the tube. Were you able to do it? Why or why not, and how is this exercise an analogy for the consequences of sin?

Discuss

–   How do your sins affect you? How do they affect your relationships with others? How do they affect your relationship with God?

–   Why should confessing sin be a part of our prayers?

–   What is the difference between feeling guilt and shame? Why is this an important distinction?

–   Parents: It's important for you to model remorse and repentance for your kids. Talk about a time when you sinned and tried to hide it from God and from others. What was that experience like for you?

Week 3

Desperate

"As the deer pants for streams of water,
so my soul pants for you, my God."
Psalm 42:1

When do you think about water the most? Maybe it's after you've played outside on a hot day. Or maybe it's after you have something salty to eat. We may not think about water all of the time, but when you're really thirsty, water is probably just about *all* you can think about. And the thirstier you are, the more you'll think about it – and be grateful for it!

The writer of Psalm 42 in the Bible knew what it was like to be thirsty. He said he felt as thirsty as a deer that desperately needed a drink of water from a stream. But the psalmist wasn't merely thirsty for water. It says that he was thirsty for God (v. 2).

What does it mean to be thirsty for God? It means more than just being physically thirsty. It is a way of telling God that you need Him. It means to crave God's power and presence more than anything else in this whole world. And that's exactly how God wants it to be. He created you to depend upon Him, just like a thirsty person who aches and longs for a glass of cool water.

All of us are thirsty for something or someone that we hope will satisfy us and make us happy. And because we are sinners, we often look to the wrong things to do that for us. But here's what you need to remember: Only God will ever be able to fully quench your thirst and give you true, long-lasting joy.

Do

- Eat some salty crackers together, but don't drink any water right away. After eating, see how long it takes before you start feeling thirsty. Talk about what the experience of being thirsty feels like.

- Try to memorize today's Bible verse (Psalm 42:1) together as a family. To aid in memorizing, try writing down each word from the verse on separate sheets of paper. Then mix up the pieces of paper and take turns putting the words together in order.

Discuss

- Why do you think we tend to rely on ourselves and on others to solve our problems and to make us happy, when God is the only One who can truly satisfy us?

- Talk about what it means to be in a *desperate* situation. When have you ever felt desperate for something? When you are in a desperate situation, what does God want you to do about it?

- Do you think that God ever wants us to *not* be desperate for, or dependent upon, Him? Why or why not?

Week 4

Fervent

"Then you will call on me [God] and come and pray to me,
and I will listen to you. You will seek me and find
me when you seek me with all your heart."
Jeremiah 29:12-13

Doing something that is good and beneficial with your whole heart is better than doing it with half a heart or with no heart at all. Whether it's playing a sport, practicing an instrument, doing your chores, completing an assignment, or doing something kind for somebody else, when you do something with all your heart, it shows that you're really giving it your best effort. It shows that you really care about and are serious about your commitment to whatever you're doing or to the one for whom you're doing it.

Now think about this in relation to God. What would it look like if we were to only worship God half-heartedly? Or what if we were to do that with prayer? It would mean that we weren't giving God our very best. Or that we're distracted by other things that we think are more important.

God always deserves our full hearts and our full attention. It's important that we don't just go through the motions of prayer. That means that we should not only pray with our mouths, but also with our minds and our hearts. As you pray, it's important that you remember that you have the very special privilege of talking and listening to the God who created you and everything else in the universe.

Today's Scripture passage reminds us that, when we come to God with all of our hearts, He promises to hear our prayers and to allow us to know Him more. And the more we know God, the more we will want to continue giving Him our very best!

Do

- With adult supervision, put a pot of water on the stove and bring it to a boil. Then take the pot off of the burner. Talk together about what you observe. Explain that God wants us to have hearts that are "on fire" for Him (as opposed to cold or lukewarm hearts).

- Brainstorm ideas for different activities or situations in which the difference between giving your whole heart and giving half a heart could make a big difference. You might even consider role-playing or acting out some of these scenarios.

- As we covered in the adult workbook on the topic of Fervency, one of the ways in which people sometimes show their devotion to God is by fasting. Talk about different things from which a person can fast. Consider taking a "screen-time" fast (from TV, media, video games) together as a family for a portion of a day or even for an entire day. Talk afterwards about your experience.

Discuss

- Discuss different physical postures of prayer that are depicted in the Bible (e.g., standing, kneeling, bowing, lying prostrate, placing the head between the knees, looking up to heaven, lifting up hands). Pick one of these postures and practice it while praying together.

- Discuss ways that we can demonstrate that God has our full attention and full devotion when we are praying.

Week 5

Persistent

*"Then Jesus told his disciples a parable to show them
that they should always pray and not give up."*
Luke 18:1

How long did it take you to learn how to walk? To ride a bike? To write your name? All of these activities take time and lots of practice and patience. The key to learning to get better at doing something is persistence. Persistence means being determined and not giving up, even if it seems difficult or frustrating.

As today's verse shows us, God wants us to be persistent in prayer. Jesus told a parable to help teach His followers this very lesson. Jesus described a woman who was being mistreated every day by someone else. When the woman went to a judge to get help, the judge didn't answer her request – at least at first. But the woman persisted. She refused to take "no" for an answer. And because of her persistence, the judge eventually granted her request.

When God doesn't answer our prayers right away or in the way that we want, it's tempting to want to give up. But we need to remember that if God doesn't immediately answer our prayers, there must be a good reason why. Sometimes God doesn't answer our prayers because we ask for the wrong types of things, or for things that might be harmful to us or to others, or for things that don't please God. And sometimes God doesn't answer right away because He wants to teach us to be patient, to wait, and to learn to trust Him more.

Being persistent in prayer doesn't mean that you'll always get what you pray for, but it does mean that you believe God must have a good reason for not answering yet or something even better in store for you. So don't give up trusting Him.

Do

- Fill two clear bottles with water. Put 5-10 drops of blue food coloring into one of the bottles. Say, "This blue water is like the judge in Jesus' parable." Then put 5-10 drops of yellow food coloring into the other water bottle and say, "This yellow water represents the woman in the parable." Then using a funnel, slowly pour a little yellow water into the blue water. You likely won't see much color change occur at first. But then pour a little bit more of the yellow water into the blue water. Keep slowly adding yellow water until the water in the second bottle turns green. Ask, "How long did it take for the color change to take effect? How is this like the persistence of the woman in Jesus' parable?"

Discuss

- Talk about a time when you've asked for something over and over. What was the eventual result?

- If we always got exactly what we wanted, any time we wanted, how would we probably begin treating God?

- What can you do to encourage others to keep praying and not give up?

Week 6

Expectant

*"In the morning, Lord, you hear my voice; in the morning
I lay my requests before you and wait expectantly."*
Psalm 5:3

When you sit on a chair, what do you expect will happen? What about when you jump off of a diving board? Or when you put a seed into good soil and give it plenty of water and light?

In each of these situations, we expect certain things will happen based upon what we know to be true about chairs and gravity and how seeds grow. In some cases, the things we expect to happen will take place pretty quickly. In other cases, it may take a bit longer. In either case, though, we expect *something* to happen.

What does the Bible teach us about what you can expect to happen when you pray? There are at least four things you can be confident of:

— You can be confident that God hears you when you pray for things that please Him (1 John 5:14-15).

— You can be confident that God cares about you more than you could ever imagine (John 3:16; 1 Peter 5:7).

— You can be confident that there is nothing that God cannot do (Matthew 19:26).

— You can be confident that God always keeps His promises (Luke 1:37).

What does this mean for you? It means that you can pray every day and all throughout the day with confidence and hope and expectation. He will give you exactly what you need, exactly when you need it.

Do

- Come up with a list of predictions for things you think will happen in the future (e.g., What will the exact temperature be tomorrow? What grade will you get on your next test? Who will win the next Super Bowl? What will you be doing in 10, 20, or 30 years? What kind of cars, houses, and clothes will people own?). Discuss how the reliability of our predictions is different from whenever God makes a promise.

Discuss

- How difficult is it to be expectant when you pray? Why?

- Can you think of other truths or promises from the Bible (other than the four listed above) of which you can be confident when you pray?

- What has God taught you about prayer during this study?

About the Authors

This study guide was written collaboratively by the three teaching pastors at Bridges Community Church in Los Altos, California.

David Gudgel – Lead Pastor and Teaching Pastor

Dave is a native Californian. Prior to Bridges, he was the Senior Pastor of Agoura Bible Fellowship in Southern California for twenty-one years, and then the Senior Pastor of Bethany Bible Church in Phoenix, AZ for seven years. For the past thirty years, Dave has also taught for Walk Thru the Bible Ministries. Dave earned a BA degree in Sociology at Westmont College, a M. Div in Practical Theology from Talbot Theological Seminary, and a Doctorate in Preaching at Western Seminary. Dave has written several books including: *Owner's Guide to Using Your Bible, Before You Get Engaged, Just One More Thing: Before You Leave Home,* and *Bible StoryBoards.* Dave and his wife, Bernice, have three children and eleven grandchildren.

Steve Durand – Family Pastor and Teaching Pastor

Steve is originally from Houston, Texas. He earned his BA degree from Baylor University and a Masters of Arts in Christian Education from Southwestern Baptist Theological Seminary. Steve is passionate about encouraging and training parents and couples, as well as helping churches become more intentional about passing faith along to the next generation. He and his wife, Shannon, have three teenage children.

Dan Stockum – Young Adult Pastor and Teaching Pastor

Originally from Ohio, Dan has spent most of his life in the south, serving churches in Georgia and Alabama. He earned his Master of Divinity from Beeson Divinity School in Birmingham. Before coming to Bridges, Dan served as a campus minister at Georgia Tech (his other alma mater) for seven years. He and his wife, Beth, have two young sons.

Made in the USA
Columbia, SC
13 February 2019